DEVOTED

REVERIE

Devoted Reverie
Copyright © 2020 by Isabella G. Poetry. All rights reserved.
No part of this book may be used or reproduced without written permission
except in the case of reprints in the context of reviews.

Cover Design, Photos, Words by Isabella G. Poetry

ISBN: 9798683294472

To everyone who ever felt like
not being good enough…

…because you are ♥

A note from me to you

First of all I want to **thank you**. Thank you for picking this book up. It means a lot to me, that you want to spend some time between these pages.
I hope my words will find a way to touch you.

Writing is my way of healing and dreaming and so much more. I love to travel and the pictures in this book are from all around the world. The dreamer in me believes this book has the chance to travel farther than I ever will.

I hope to inspire you.

Please note that some of these poems contain the following topics:

>Toxic / Violent relationship
>Death of a loved one
>Addiction
>Self-Harm
>Eating disorders
>And potentially more

Remember to practice self-care.

This book is my journey. It's my love letter to poetry.

A dreamer's heart engraved on paper.

And now... let's get lost in reverie

Isabella G. Poetry

I. Beautifully Broken
II. Wanderlust
III. Dreaming Wide Awake
IV. Shards Of A Healing Heart

INTRO

Through the rain
Let the symphony rise
Despite the pain
This is devoted reverie

A heart uncaged
Onto the page it bleeds
Creating art to get assuaged
This is devoted reverie

BEAUTIFULLY
BROKEN

My brokenness use to be my downfall
Now I embrace each shard of my he**art**
Because I am still here after it all
Seeing now how my heart's made up of **art**

These scars are my diary
You can't erase them from my skin
If they disappeared
There would be no me

We killed the monsters
From our past
In their places slowly emerge
Much worse beasts

Our hands were tired
Of holding on
As our hearts grew tired
Of being alone

Isabella G. Poetry

Our Love
It was built to fall
Fated to break
And to crack apart

If destiny should be enough
Tell me why
It's not working for us
It's a lie
That extraordinary love
Can happen twice

I was wrong
Such a fool
Thinking you'd
Tell the truth
Believed our love
Was bulletproof

WHY NOT US

We sacrificed so much
Almost everything
There's nothing left to give
But dust and air
If they could make it
Why not us?

Why is this love not enough?
Why were we destined to fail
If we started so beautiful?
Why is this love consumed by pain?
Why were we designed so frail
If we started so strong?

Why did all our tries
End in misery?
Realization cuts like a knife
It's so unfair
When they could make it
Why not us?

Why is this love not enough?
Why were we destined to fail
If we started so beautiful?
Why is this love consumed by pain?
Why were we designed so frail
If we started so strong?

Why were we destined to fail?
Why were we designed so frail?
If they are strong enough
Tell me, why not us?

The most beautiful lie
Was that everything would be fine
When truthfully this life denied
For us to have more time

If muscle memory exists
My heart will never learn
How to unlove you

If muscle memory exists
I will survive this
Because it's all I have ever done

Adele sang I'll find someone like you
But I don't think that's possible
And Ari said there are no tears left to cry
But I am not sure I am there yet

We were messy
But we were us
We were perfect
But 'we' are past

Shopping for a new heart
Looking for what's on sale
Strolling with my empty cart
Realizing I should have never given mine away

My heart had darkened
Like a starless night
I wear the shadows in my scars

But

Now that I am broken
The embers can ignite
And light can shine through the cracks

Isabella G. Poetry

Balancing on breaking ruins
While outrunning the past
Watching dreams go up in flames
With no time to rest

Balancing on sharp edges
While I wipe tears off my face
Running despite consequences
With no intention to look back

Inside of her is a lost soul
Give some love to her
Since her smile's already resold
To the highest bidder

These eyes use to laugh
They use to hold the light of a thousand fires
Now the spark has grown cold
Waves of sadness run rivers down her chin

These eyes use to be kind
They use to be warm like midsummer rain
Now the summer left for snow
Waves of anger leave bleeding traces on her skin

Isabella G. Poetry

You twist words
To lies
Like poison ivy

Thinking this'll shine
A light of glory
Down on you

You're so blinded
You can't even see
The irony

Don't tell me to smile more
This will just turn me sour

The harder I want to let go
The harder it gets to forget
Trying to let this breath out
Because if anything…
… I don't want to feel regrets

I don't want to pretend
Like I am letting you in
Because we both know
How this is going to end

You build me up
To watch me fall
You break my soul apart
Let my mind go insane
Let my senses bleed
And bury all that's left of me

In your hands my strength
Became my downfall
When love turned into war
And soft hands turned skin black and blue

There were things I did wrong
I will admit to it all
But it should have never led to this
To all these wounds and bruises

In your hands my heart
The avalanche of happiness
The spring of my creativeness
Became an empty place

Take me back to way back when
It all use to make sense
Life seemed so much easier then
Now it's all just pretend

If I'd have to choose
Between the poison of your love
Or to die alone
My choice would always be you

Isabella G. Poetry

You are like a wave
Washing over me
Ready to pull me under
To watch me drown
Just to pull me out
And pretend
You saved me

You are my cruel remedy
Rising like a symphony
Healing me
Just to break me

Isabella G. Poetry

THE RAIN

It's been days, yet I can't call this a memory
The rain is still pouring down on me
Hope and light still a faraway reverie
Whilst you pour the rain over me

You've tried and tried to wash it away
But your fingerprints are left on me
Run, run away this will chase you down
It's what you get for letting me drown

Been trying to get up today
But you've taken the power out of me
Run, run away with a guilty soul
My skin is prove and my blood is on you

It's been days, yet I can't call this a memory
The rain is still pouring down on me
Hope and light still a faraway reverie
Whilst you pour the rain over me

The stains on my soul are still raw
Don't complain about the rain you caused
Run, run away this will chase you down
You've got nowhere to hide, it's pouring

Come on, face what you've done
Just like mine your soul is damned
Run, run away with a guilty soul
This will haunt you my blood is on you

Isabella G. Poetry

It's been days, yet I can't call this a memory
The rain is still pouring down on me
Hope and light still a faraway reverie
Whilst you pour the rain over me

Don't complain
Because you've caused the rain
You'll pay for what you've done
Because no one outruns the rain

I won't rescue you
Cause you'll just desert me
I won't put you on a pedestal no more
Cause now I see what you are made of

Somehow you've stolen it all
The light from the sun
The words from each song
You make the world feel empty
Are you proud now?

I am bleeding out
Do you see me now?

I have been screaming out
Do you hear me now?

I am crawling back to life
Now you want to help out?

                                    I have survived alone
                                    Won't need you anymore

Humans experience tragedy
We break as we live
And we hurt as we try to love
We wrap our hearts in safety
As we try to conquer life
And we fail to keep our hearts from breaking

When it was good it was great
But when things went wrong
I was fully defeated

You threw me into the gutter
Made sure I would feel unloved
But I got back up

When you least expected it
I gathered all my strength
And rose to the top

My exile became my queendom

I never told you not to love her
Always knew you had a good heart
Don't worry about what happens to me
Surely she'll kiss away your hurt

Watch the fire burning
The ashes are your letters
Watch how it's growing
The embers are the forevers

You see scars
I see stories
You see weakness
Born from vain
I see strength
Born from pain

They call it a pride of lions
And an unkindness of ravens
So I wonder what's the name
For doomed lovers like us

Isabella G. Poetry

They say
Don't trust anything living under the sun
Maybe that's why
I feel most alive and safest under the moon

Never want to show
The storm inside my mind
Time can heal but this won't
This raging tempest is too strong

You fall by the wayside
Feel like dust to other people's eyes
Worthless is how you feel inside
You always try to hide the pain with a smile

I have fought for your approval
Been bending myself to fit your mold
I will never be close to good enough

Kept going despite it all
Wasted so much time in denial
Can't even recognize myself in the mirror

Under your thumb
I can't breathe
Feeling numb
Trying to fight myself free

Love crumbles between your hands
You flood my eyes with tears
But the worst part is
You enjoy the misery you bring

You're the destroyer of worlds
The catcher of dreams
Monsters envy you
Nothing escapes your hands alive

Even your presence is a warning sign
The devil would trade his demons for you
All you ever do is spread emotional famine
The laws of war mean nothing to you

Thief of hearts
Give back
The love I saved
For myself

You said you felt like my heart
Had ran out of room for you
When really all it ever did
Was beat solely for you
I am sorry for not showing you
For not loving you the way I should
I promise I did all I could

I want to flip the page
Start a new
But what are you supposed to do
When there are no pages left

Isabella G. Poetry

HALOS (WHO WE ARE)

As we wander
Between street lights
That shine gently down on us
We wonder who we are

We question
What makes us human
Yet there are no answers
Between the stars

We see most halos
Are just reflections from the rain
For a heart that has known pain
Now radiates with love

As we wander
On dusty old roads
With the most beautiful views
We wonder who we are

Too many questions
For one life to find all answers
We keep being children
In the arms of mother earth

We see most halos
Are just reflections from the rain
For a heart that has known pain
Now radiates with love

Isabella G. Poetry

As we wander
On breaking pavements
With outworn shoes
We wonder who we are

This world might be
Ours for the taking
But when we're gone
What will remain?

We see most halos
Are just reflections from the rain
As street lights
Shine gently down on us

Isabella G. Poetry

Cotton candy clouds
Paint the sky beautifully
Do you ever look down?
I want to make you proud
Still miss you terribly
Always felt safest in your sound

When people we love
Leave
We're left with nothing
But grief

It will take time
To see
We're all our own
Scar collective

These are the scars
That unmask the past
And unravel my heart

Isabella G. Poetry

> I mostly know you through photographs
>
> To get close, life and death denied
>
> One day I'll see you perhaps
>
> I hope you'll welcome me with arms wide

It's been years
Since you left
But my heart seems
Not to care

So I am
Drowning in grief
Until we meet
Again

I still get teary thinking of you
How I felt save in your arms
The way we use to laugh
I wish cancer hadn't taken you so soon

Isabella G. Poetry

You left this world too soon
I wish I could still be cradled by you
I wish I could still see you, speak to you
Instead all I have is a gravestone

Life didn't always treat you right
I know you know loss inside out
If there were words to find
I would say them but there are none

BURDEN

This should have never been your role
This weight should have never been yours to hold
Because this darkness took your hope
And now you feel buried underneath this burden
You're falling faster than you know
Might never get to see your future unfold

Long gone are days the darkness only crept in
Now it's an old friend tapping your shoulder
Never far behind you

Holding on, barely
Keep going, slowly
Shallow breathing
This weight is suffocating you
Wanting to live, eagerly
Escaping, desperately
The walls of safety
Are crumbling down

It has become the only thing you know
The winter snow inside your heart is too cold
Your dreams are frozen and on hold
Now you feel buried underneath this burden
Time became sand between your hands
Moving faster than quicksand

Long gone are days the darkness only crept in
Now it's an old friend through thick and thin
Always right beside you

Holding on, barely
Keep going, slowly
Shallow breathing
This weight is suffocating you
Wanting to live, eagerly
Escaping, desperately
The walls of safety
Are crumbling down

Long gone are the days your face knew how to smile
This world became a sadder place that day
When your life left your heart
And darkness crept in

Holding on, barely
Keep going, slowly
Shallow breathing
This weight is suffocating you
Wanting to live, eagerly
Escaping, desperately
The walls of safety
Are crumbling down

Now these ruins became a graveyard
I hope among the stars you'll shine
With a light weighted heart
And the happiness this life denied

Isabella G. Poetry

If grief is supposed to get easier with time
Why does each passing day
Hurt more and more
And more

And here I am
                        Leaving every single door unlocked
                           Every window slightly open
                                  Just in hopes
                               You'll come back

Isabella G. Poetry

There's no expiration date to grieve
Don't let anyone tell you otherwise
Not even your own heart

Isabella G. Poetry

Dear Bridgett
Thank you for putting Soft Thorns out into the world
Now lost souls like mine can find your words ♥

7th Circle of Hell

Burning raindrops fall from the sky
Violence rules this no-man's-land
The desert beneath our feet's on fire
Embers and coal dust our hands

Pouring rain won't wash the hurt away
The bleeding hearts are about to burst
Knowing the enemy is right there in the mirror
Falling faster, hitting ground, all at the same time

Screaming voices, whispers, cries
Nothing will wash the blood from these hands
If you say differently you're a liar
Even with running we won't stand a chance

Pouring rain won't wash the hurt away
The bleeding hearts are about to burst
Knowing the enemy is right there in the mirror
Falling faster, hitting ground, all at the same time

WANDERLUST

Take me on the road
This heart wasn't made
To stay in one place

Isabella G. Poetry

My heart is an island
You have to learn how to swim
Fight with me through storms ahead
But once you are in
I will give you everything

I love open water
The freedom to swim anywhere
I admire the darkest forests
The freedom to hide secrets between trees
I feel content when travelling
The freedom to let your heart out into the wild

Sometimes I wonder if my love to travel
Stems from wanting to touch the sky
To once again feel close to you
Even if it's just for a while

Strolling on the beach
Feet in the water
Walking through the streets
Nightlights above us

- Perfect day

Isabella G. Poetry

Late nights
Walking on cobblestone streets
Hand in hand as we laugh among friends
Cheers to the night, fullest hearts
Only witnesses are the lake, the cloudy sky
And you

- Dear Zürich

As dusk starts its beautiful chorus
We watch hail pour
While the starry nights falls

Let demons crawl out of shadows
Because we know
Nothing can truly stop us

Knowing and loving
People in more than one place
Will always make your heart ache
In the most beautiful way

Isabella G. Poetry

One day the girl got on a plane
Oblivious to the journey ahead
She was afraid of the unknown
But now sees life through a different lens

When the girl got off the plane
She feared loneliness but instead
Crossed path with warm hearted souls
She would one day call friends

To Masumi, Jinmi, Jasmin,
Michelle, Javi and Corina
I am grateful for all of you ♥

Isn't it beautiful
How a stranger's soul
Can be the one
You've been waiting for

Isabella G. Poetry

Lost between pages
Home in thousands of worlds
Flipping the pages
New adventures ahead

Isabella G. Poetry

Watching you leave
I see this love I can't retrieve
My unchained melody
Sinking in this deep sea

Take me somewhere
Anywhere
Wherever this hurt
Will be less

Paths part
Stories end
A new start
Same broken heart

I am not running away
I am collecting parts of me
From around the world
I never knew I lost

Isabella G. Poetry

Spin the globe
Wherever your finger lands
We'll go
And take on the adventure
We'll pack our love
Won't need anything else

Her soul was free
Never made
To live in one place
Never to be tamed

Walking on this old dirt road
Finding pieces you threw away
Slowly putting myself back together
Maybe messily but beautifully me

Isabella G. Poetry

Put a vinyl record on
I want to get lost
To some old song
Right here with you

Who once was a stranger
Can become your closest companion
Sometimes just for a chapter
But sometimes for the whole story

You're a warm light
In a cold night
Shining bright
To lead me home

Isabella G. Poetry

They say we come into this world alone
But I can feel you've started the way I walk
You're not around to ask where to go anymore
But I can still feel you taking care of me

Her restless heart
Will only find release
When it can explore
And learn more

Isabella G. Poetry

Washed up at shore
Sand between my toes
Feeling free
Feeling at home

We had nothing to give, but our love
Kisses were our currency
We had no money, but were so rich
Our hearts felt free

I love to travel by train

See the world pass by

Nothing on my mind

Just soaking it all in

There's beauty in longing
Just like there's beauty in finally finding

Isabella G. Poetry

A whole summer
Feeling on top of the world
Met so many amazing people
Made so many precious memories
I keep them close to my heart
Just like you... and all the beauty you hold

- Dear Vancouver

When travelling alone
Your heart will unlace
You will never be
Lost

You will find more
Than beautiful places
You will find
You

All this time
Just to find
Home is not a place
But a feeling

All this time
Beautiful views
Love filled heart
My home is travelling

Isabella G. Poetry

Jet Lag:
80% mindset
10% caffeine
10% dreaming

- A travel lover's advice

The heart does not know distance.
You can feel connected to someone halfway
around the world…

                … and miss someone right next to you.

Explore with me
The unknown
The unseen
The new

Create with me
Love
Tenderness
The present

Explore with me
My soul
My heart
The old

Share with me
Your darkness
Your happiness
All that is you

Create with me
Memories
Smile lines
The future

Isabella G. Poetry

This heart aches to explore
Wants to find the beauty in everything
Wants to taste the foods from everywhere
Wants to stroll along rivers anywhere

This heart will never be content
Contained in one place

DREAMING
WIDE AWAKE

My scars tell stories
That'll never leave my lips

Scarred from the past

                                        But still not scared to get scars

As my tears
Slowly fall
They end up as ink
On a paper sheet

Your love wore thin
You're not worth it
You and all this pain
I will leave behind

I am so delicate
I am about to break
You made me weak
                        My future is up for debate
                             Who I was is undone
                        And who I am is unknown

I see you over there
Just a breath away from me
So close
But yet so far
Because it's not me
You're taking home tonight

When 3 am turns into a feeling
Rather than a time
I might have been thinking
For a bit too long

Our love was like an hourglass
We saw the sand run out
Tried to catch it between our hands
But time ran out too fast

Isabella G. Poetry

When the hail is too strong
And your vision is blurred
Be your own shelter
Build an umbrella

Even frozen rain is an obstacle
We are capable to endure
So go ahead heart
Reach for your stars

While you sleep
I'll build the castle of our dreams
Just you and me
Wrapped in a love that gleams

Isabella G. Poetry

Unbeknownst to you
You hold a soul
With a spark
That causes lanterns to light
Sending shockwaves
Through my heart

Time let us drift apart
More than miles are between us now
But you're still close to my heart
I hope your dreams came true

Isabella G. Poetry

I never quite knew
If you were flying or falling
It was almost like a whisper
Only the wind could hear
Wherever life has taken you
I hope you soar

Isabella G. Poetry

When the tide is rising
Watch the waves come in
They will wash away the pain
And make space to breath

I first fell in love
With poetry
The day I read Milk & Honey
By Rupi Kaur
Page eighteen
And forever my love will bloom

Pitting us against each other
Writing jealousy into our stories
Will never reflect our truth
Because we are stronger than they want us to believe

- Women supporting women

'Be smart' they say
'Be pretty' they say
Be a little too much of these things
And they'll fear you

- so be all YOU want to be

'Wear nice things' they say
'But don't show too much skin'
'This is not appropriate' they say
'But you should put more effort in'

- wear what you feel CONFIDENT in

Isabella G. Poetry

Reminisce with me
About the good times
Before the mistakes
And heart aches

I want human connections
Love, friendships, even strangers
Just feeling connected for a second
In a world that's superficial

Isabella G. Poetry

You've tried to hurt me with your words
Tried to silence me with your hands
But darling,
You've only seen the cage
That holds the lioness inside of me

- Lionheart

There's a fire
Burning underneath my skin
It's a desire
Running through my bloodstream

You can try to tear me down
But I will get back up
Even if it is the long way around
I will find solid ground

I will ignite my fire
The desire inside my soul
I will ignite my strength
It is all inside of me

- Temperature rising

By trying to steal my light
You'll just get burned
I've worked for it
So I got resistant to the flames

Isabella G. Poetry

You're like a lavender field
Mysteriously beautiful
While you try to hide your lies
Between all shades of purple

Isabella G. Poetry

Vultures circle above you
Like a dark halo
You're on your throne of thorns
Reign a land of coals

How deep your words slash
You'll never know
A hollow soul like yours
Can't fathom the sorrow

You say I am causing my own pain
As you twist the knife deeper in

You coldly avoid my tears
Like they don't stain the sheets
On which you lay
Your head to sleep

Burning bridges tonight
Dancing between the embers
Soaking up the light
Using the past as kerosene

Isabella G. Poetry

You might see falling petals
I see new space for growth

Words flood out my finger tips
Just like tears fall from my chin
These poems are my rebirth
As I let go of what once was

This love is a sweet temptation
As we dance around this fire
This feeling is what I have desired
I have no choice but to surrender

Kiss me to sleep
With an angels touch
So the devil in me
Can't light his torch

Isabella G. Poetry

We're growing apart
But we pull it together
All these lies for a start
We'll come clean about

My heart can't do without
What we use to be
We both played our parts
We can't do this forever

Have to forgive for a start
Taking this new route
'cause my heart can't do without
What we could be

Give me one last dance, please
Before all of this turns into a memory
For one more song I want to feel alive
Before all of this turns into a sad story

As we know the end is coming
We try and make it beautiful
Make some last few memories
Engrave them in our hearts

Isabella G. Poetry

After everything that has been
Goodbye should be the easy part
You still get under my skin
And I can't numb my heart

I just can't let go
After holding on for so long

You were the best part of me
If the two of us were a rose
You would be the beautiful petals
Because I am only made up of thorns

A dying rose
Still has her thorns
While new petals
Emerge

A crashing wave
Still holds power
While the next one
Grows

Isabella G. Poetry

Before the black sky turns into blue
Before the moon kisses the wide horizon
I will go and find you

When the tides rising waves crash onto shore
When the peonies have started their full bloom
That's when I'll finally hold you

Warm summer nights
Dark skies
Fragile hearts
With determined minds

We will nurture this soil
Leave behind the turmoil
Redefine our status quo
So good love can grow

I remember watching you go
Still wish I would've had the strength to reach out
And tell you not to leave
But that will remain a dream

If you never risk
Then you'll never know
If you never fall
Then you'll never bruise
But are you truly alive
If you never hurt?
It is part of this life
It is part of growth

Let courage carry you
Even if it's a wild ride
Don't become a coward
You can't go back in time

Your sparkling eyes
Illumine the night
I am just wondering
If it's from tears or smiles

Laughing brightly
Dancing slowly
Same old story
Ending tragically

Isabella G. Poetry

Now we've got nothing to loose
It's just me and you
Let's dive deep between the waves
Deep down we're safe

Your heartbeat is my favorite lullaby
With you I'll get through every night
My demons seem smaller
With you by my side

Neon lights
Reflect in your eyes
Night air around us
Creating our own paradise

Even when
We are apart
We're holding hands
Through our hearts

SOUND TO THE SONG

It's been too long
I can't remember your smile
It's been months
I can't remember your voice

Yet here you are
Right there, so come closer
Put your arms around my chest, tightly
Want to breathe you in
Just like it's supposed to be
These arms will always be home to me

Within a breath time is nonexistent anymore
We've been apart but your lips are so familiar
You are the lighthouse in my darkness
The one that puts the sound into the song
Who solidifies my trembling ground

If one falls
A hand gets extended
We will rise
For together we are strongest

And here you are
Right there, so come closer
Put your arms around my chest, tightly
Want to breathe you in
Just like it's supposed to be
These arms will always be home to me

We both have our own set of wings but for as long
As I fly I will always catch your breeze
Our hands extend our hearts
As they hold on like there is no time left
For right now is all we have got

So now here you are
Right there, so come closer
Put your arms around my chest, tightly
Want to breathe you in
Just like it's supposed to be
These arms

These arms
Will always be
Always be
Home to me

Wild embers
Creating sparks
Slowly dancing
Between our hearts

Isabella G. Poetry

Your breath on my lips
Your skin under my fingertips
Heaven between sheets
Even if half of it is just a dream

If I could go back
I wouldn't hesitate
Wouldn't wait
But you are gone
And '**I love you**' died
On my lips

Turns out, I never needed to be fixed
Should have never believed your words
Instead of accepting myself

Turns out, your words were lies
They might have scarred my soul
But they have never truly destroyed me

Sorry,
But it turns out
I am stronger than your cruelty

Isabella G. Poetry

A dash of naïveté
A pinch of tenderness
With a cup of creativity
And a whole jar of messiness

- Ingredients of my heart

SHARDS OF A
HEALING HEART

When the hurt
Gets replaced
The past
Gets erased

We try to learn
But instead repeat
The same
Mistakes

A neglected heart is still a beating heart

                    A breaking heart will become a healing heart

The pavements beneath my soles
Are the remnants of the old
Scaring me like hot coals
But today, I finally leave this road

I have never walked a longer road
Than this one

It's filled with stones, pain and thorns
It's filled with love, light and laughter

I have never walked a longer road
Than the one to forgiving myself

What I once thought
Would shatter my bones
Is now one of the bravest chapters
I have survived

Isabella G. Poetry

You've pulled me out of the darkness
Gave me light during painful times
Showed me when I was begging for forgiveness
All I needed was to write my rhymes

Thank you poetry
For saving me

This madness
Is a sweet remedy
Compared to the painful rage
That came before

I don't need you to save me
My broken heart is my canvas
If you can't handle me
You'll only get cut by my shards

One day this chaotic heart
Will have the power
To fuel the burning embers
And create art

Most people don't understand you
Because they haven't met you
They haven't heard your whispers
Don't know how to listen

They won't understand it all
Even if some try really hard
It took years for me to let you go
But it was time to move on

Overcoming you was learning
And accepting and restarting
And hurting and breaking
And crying and healing

Maybe one day
You won't be more
Than a word
To me

Bulimia
You almost ruined me

But only
Almost

Close to you I never knew
How toxic you were
But from a distance
The veil's see-through

ADDICTION

My soul is craving darkness
Like a never ending hunger
I run back to what I tried to escape
With you I become fearless
If I am prey, you're the hunter
The darkness within me awakes

You hear me, never judge me
You're a beauty, yet might kill me

You're my first thought in the morning
The blissful feeling I long to hold onto
This knowing of faithful understanding
I am spiraling into your arms
A willing lover to the hardships and burden
Your love isn't priceless but it's pure
When the world gets loud and overwhelming
You lead the way and collect all the shards
Of what little that had been left of me

You drown out the whole world
Pain gets numb and the tears stop falling
All that I was gets erased
Because you leave me burned
You seem to control and consume me
The darkness within me awakes

You comfort me, never leave me
You're a mastermind of manipulation

You're my first thought in the morning
The blissful feeling I long to hold onto
This knowing of faithful understanding
I am spiraling into your arms

A willing lover to the hardships and burden
Your love isn't priceless but it's pure
When the world gets loud and overwhelming
You lead the way and collect all the shards
Of what little that had been left of me

My soul is craving light
Not sure where I can find it
But I am deserving of healing
Healing from you

Isabella G. Poetry

Tidal waves crash against the shore
Sinking among the stones are the shards of my heart
I won't need them anymore
In their place more beautiful things have grown

Amongst the chaos I'll be fine
No need to fear
Because if I am torn
I am still alive

Between the chaos I am fine
Still on the battleground
No fight is lost
Until you stop to try

Isabella G. Poetry

I am scared of the hope inside of me
My heart and mind speak in riddles I can't comprehend
This time I won't fight the growing peace
Surrender fully and let my heart rule over my head

This battleground has been the soil
To the uprising of my soul

Shaped by a cruel world
She learned how to survive
All the pain you threw at her
And still she thrives

Isabella G. Poetry

Even a delicate flower
Can withstand storms
As softness holds the power
To change its form

For some time
'I'm sorry'
Was what I
Was craving to hear
But as I grow older
I've come to see
You are not capable
To say these words

Your imperfections are what make you whole
They are part of what make you beautiful
You've got a kind heart and a warrior's soul
They are the foundation for you to evolve

Please take care of yourself
Our paths won't be intertwined no more
Our book is done, sitting on a shelf
But I still wish you only good

Isabella G. Poetry

In this life
There went so much wrong
In between the laughs

You were
Always a long way from home
But never really lost

And I hope
Wherever it is you now go
It will be a kinder place

You've come so far
In so many ways you've grown
But all you ever gaze upon
Is the dirt on your road

I hope one day you'll see
All the beauty and gold
You leave behind
In other people's souls

In the darkest hours
I collect myself
And fuel my power

This heart
Is too much of a rebel
To just give up

No one has the power to tear me down like you

No one has the energy to punch me when I am on the ground like you

No one has the ability to put negative thoughts inside my head like you

But I have the power to destroy you, too.

- Note to negative self

Give me thunder
Give me hail
Give me rain storms
Give me pain

Whatever you throw
I'll get through

Isabella G. Poetry

A rose lattice around my heart
Protective thorns
Soft petals
A heart not quite ready to love again

I was afraid to step into the unknown
But one thing my scars have taught me
Is how I am so much stronger
Than the girl I was believed she could be

SOLITUDE

This reverie is the ground I am walking on
2 hours of sleep are enough
When I am drunk on these dreams
For they hold the future I will craft
I might not fit into the box
You created for me
Because I am more than one thing

I will always have reverie
Running through my bloodstream
So when death decides to take me
I hope the devil will hate me
Because I went after my dreams
Knowing how time never goes slowly
Didn't put my story on hold
Dreams don't fall from the sky
And if I have to walk this road in solitude
My dreams are worth it, life's too short

This reverie is the foundation I am built upon
My heart is wild with desire
You can't please the crowds
Their boxes aren't made for us
What's yours will find you
And what's mine will come
Just keep working hard

I will always have reverie
Running through my bloodstream
So when death decides to take me
I hope the devil will hate me

Because I went after my dreams
Knowing how time never goes slowly
Didn't put my story on hold
Dreams don't fall from the sky
And if I have to walk this road in solitude
My dreams are worth it, life's too short

This reverie is what sets my soul on fire
Society is not who I aim to please
Will never bend to fit their molds
If you don't understand that's fine
Our differences should be embraced
Life's rough enough
We can't limit our growth
Our souls are meant to be free

I will always have reverie
Running through my bloodstream
So when death decides to take me
I hope the devil will hate me
Because I went after my dreams
Knowing how time never goes slowly
Didn't put my story on hold
Dreams don't fall from the sky
And if I have to walk this road in solitude
My dreams are worth it, life's too short

I will always have reverie
Running through my bloodstream
Even if I walk in solitude
Because reverie is the ground I am walking on

Isabella G. Poetry

This pain will die in vain
When the rain has cleared the clouds
Because this heart will remain
Beating with the strength of a thousand suns

After everything you've put me through
It's not like me to fear the fall anymore
I am so much stronger, thanks to you
Won't let anyone hurt me like you

Isabella G. Poetry

You are 68 years older than me
I still remember how my little hand
Fitted softly into your wrinkled one
I looked up to you then

I wonder what your eyes have seen
In your 95 years down here
One thing I hope you know
Is how I never stop looking up to you

Only the last few years
Of your life
Did I really get to know you and spend time with you

I am writing with tears
In my eyes
Because I loved getting to know you more

When the hurt clears
I know I
Will always smile when I think of you

Your soul might have left
Your body
But you will never disappear out of our hearts

I never got to tell you
All of this
I hope you somehow know how much I still care

Sometimes I remember your voice
Want to hold on to it
Before it fades into silence again

Sometimes I remember your smell
Want to close my eyes
And want to take the deepest breaths

Sometimes I know you are here
You left this world years ago
But my heart can still feel you're near

The other day
I found a letter from you
Seeing my name
In your cursive writing

Teary eyed
I remember
Your hands touched
This old paper

Holding it now
Is like I am
Holding your hand
Again

Isabella G. Poetry

Keeping my eyes on the coast line
Taking my heart out of its coffin
Scared to bring it back to life

But reminded how one
Can only loose
If one has truly loved

While I was falling apart
You sat there, front row
I finally finished my part
And it's time for you to go

Isabella G. Poetry

I never needed to be hard as stone
Most beautiful things come and go
They continue to grow
Adapt with their softness to the hardness of this world

I never needed to be the never ending storm
Most beautiful waters have the tide come and go
Just like rivers flow
They adapt their waters to the storms of this world

Hold me close
But don't hold me down
Walk with me
Don't pull me along

It might feel
Like breaking down
You might just need
A little break
Or a change of perspective
Before you can see
You are close to
Breaking through

Isabella G. Poetry

I love midsummer rain
It's music to my skin
My hearts poetry
And my soul's medicine

Redemption will find your soul
One day you will start healing
Never give up on yourself
Your soul will find **redemption**

The feather you blew away
The one you tried so hard to destroy
Grew the wings
That make me soar today

Been looking for a light
To lead me

And bring me to safety
Could never see

The potential fire
Deep within me

Learned from all the pain
How to ignite it

I couldn't see the embers were
Inside of me

We are like storms
Sometimes a bit messy
Rough from time to time
But always powerful

Isabella G. Poetry

FLOWER CROWNS

Look at the ruins
From which we've grown
They want to see us fail
As we rise above pain
They tried to take our hope
But what they don't know
There is always a light
That leads us home

The only thing we know
Is to always lead with love

These scars are our armor
Our past won't be forgotten
As we emerge from battlegrounds
We wear our flower crowns
Look at the broken ruins
From which we've grown
The ashes in the dirty soil
Grew our flower crowns

Free are our thoughts
Never fueled by greed
We try to do our part
To wrap every single heart
We encounter in warmth
The cold has spread enough
Reign with love in our hearts
Even when they try to take our hope

We learned from our pain
To always lead with love

Isabella G. Poetry

These scars are our armor
Our past won't be forgotten
As we emerge from battlegrounds
We wear our flower crowns
Look at the broken ruins
From which we've grown
The ashes in the dirty soil
Grew our flower crowns

Just because we change the road
Does not mean we change the goal
It remains the same
To always lead with love

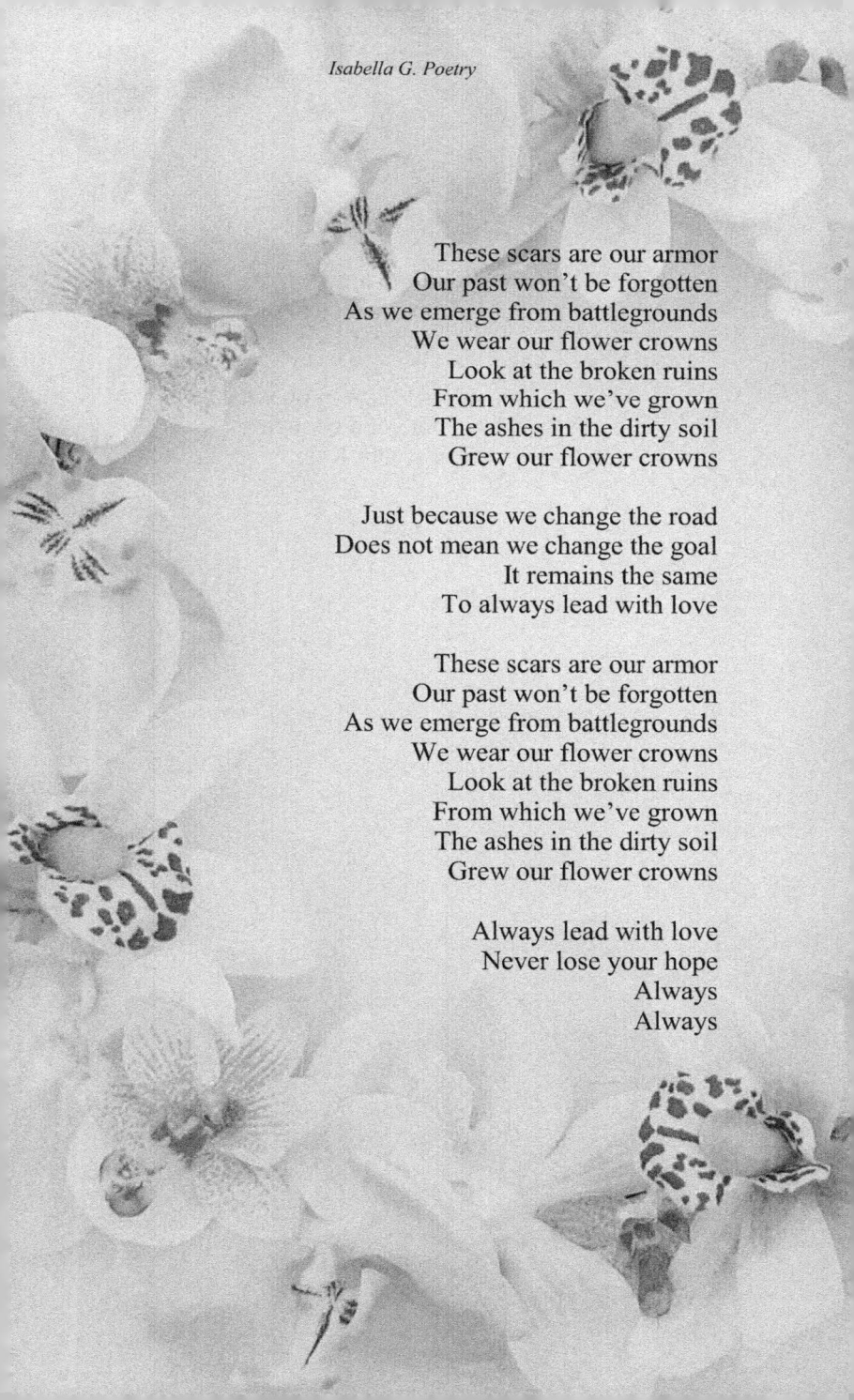

These scars are our armor
Our past won't be forgotten
As we emerge from battlegrounds
We wear our flower crowns
Look at the broken ruins
From which we've grown
The ashes in the dirty soil
Grew our flower crowns

Always lead with love
Never lose your hope
Always
Always

These scars I will no longer try to hide
If I am not good enough
So be it

Can't live holding this pain on the inside
If I am not good enough
That's your loss

Isabella G. Poetry

Writing it all down
Is my way of screaming out loud

Isobella G. Poetry

Amongst the evening crowd
At a concert we sing along
Lighters in the air
One song
A thousand hearts unite
We're arm in arm
More than elsewhere
This is home

This heart is wide open
Maybe a little vulnerable

This heart loves without
Any borders

This heart loves you
As you are

SHADES OF LAUGHTER

When my days are counted
Right before my breath will end
If I can get the chance to reminisce
Then these are the days I want to relive

Every single shade of laughter
Every shared tear of sadness
All the memories we made along the way
How we picked up the shards of our hearts
How we'd dance through starry nights
Makes me see it's not bad to be me

Whether we cried through the hurt
Or simply laughed until we cried
Every tear is a memory I treasure
This kind of love you cannot measure

Every single shade of laughter
Every shared tear of sadness
All the memories we made along the way
How we picked up the shards of our hearts
How we'd dance through starry nights
Makes me see it's not bad to be me

When my days are counted
And I remember all of this
I hope it'll make me smile
Because it's not bad to be me

Isabella G. Poetry

you paint my dreams to life

and put my hurt to rest

We've built a palace between ruins
Washed it clean with our tears
Grew stronger during our pursuit
To build for once something that lasts

Explore my heart with your soul
Trace my scars with soft hands
Give me time to stitch up my wounds
And I will pour out my love for you

I will always have a wild touch
Won't be fully yours
Because I am mine first
As I respectfully love you

Isabella G. Poetry

Now I am turning blood into ink
Breathing easier and sleeping deeper
Watching my old habits sink
Into the depth of the waters

Isabella G. Poetry

BATTLE SYMPHONY

You shall turn this battle cry
Into a symphony
Let it rise like the tides of an ocean
Coming in with full force

What use to be all consuming pain
Is now a memory that starts to fade
Because even if we break down
We will never be too torn to heal
As life goes on and love is lost
Our hearts will mend in time

Fight on, for a little longer
Hold on, just a bit longer
Because

You shall turn this battle cry
Into a symphony
Let it rise like the tides of an ocean
Coming in with full force

Like a thunder rolling through the night
You hold so much beauty deep inside
Amongst the power you try to hide
But one day it will see the light
Your presence here is needed
Hurt and pain will mend in time

Fight on, for a little longer
Hold on, just a bit longer
Because

Isabella G. Poetry

You shall turn this battle cry
Into a symphony
Let it rise like the tides of an ocean
Coming in with full force

One day, darling
Your symphony will rise
Your battle cry
Is your heartbeat

So, darling
Hold a hand to your chest
This is your battle cry
Feel each beat

Now, darling
Fight on, for a little longer
Rise like the tides of an ocean
Coming in with full force

Isabella G. Poetry

When I am fighting my inner demons
Your arms are my strongest armor

Isabella G. Poetry

The deeper the water goes
The more I want to dip my toes
I wasn't made to swim in the shallows
My soul craves deeper oceans

Isabella G. Poetry

We are all a little bit scarred
Maybe a little bit scared

We are all a little bit flawed
Maybe a little bit insecure

We are all a little bit hurt
Maybe a little bit lost

We are all warriors

Words can turn into the cruelest weapons
They can cut so deeply
Hurt so badly

Words leave scars no one can gaze upon
They are hidden from the eye
Give yourself time

Speak to yourself with kind words
Maybe you don't see it now
But you deserve love

How come
You've never tried to spread your wings?
Has the heart in your chest grown cold?
Is there nothing left but stone?

There's still a kindness to your eyes
And so I whisper a little prayer to the wind
Hoping it might catch you before you're told
How you are worthless and unlovable

From a young age all you knew was hurt
Seeing yourself smile in old pictures still makes you cry
Because this person seems to live a different life
I hope wherever you are your smile never left your lips

There's still a kindness to your eyes
And so I whisper a little prayer to the wind
Hoping it might catch you before you're told
How you are worthless and unlovable

The pain has changed your life but not your name
The scars won't be washed away
There's a strength you grew from all the falls
And just wait, one day you will see the same

OUTRO

This heart's made up of poetry
It will always watch the sea
Wondering to find release
In devoted reverie

Our souls are made up of art
Looking for canvasses to paint
Wondering to find peace
In devoted reverie

Acknowledgements:

To the ones who broke me:
It all makes sense now. Thank you for the lessons.

To the ones who laugh with me:
I am grateful to call you my friends.
I would be lost without you.

To the ones who have been there for me:
No words will ever be enough to tell you how much
I appreciate you.

To the ones who were taken too soon:
I miss you, every day. I hope I make you proud.
I love you. Always.

To Bridgett Devoue:
Thank you for showing me how the softest petals truly are
the strongest ones.

To you, dear reader:
You are holding a shard of my heart.
Thank you for reading it.
Words fail to express how much this means to me.
Thank you for your time.
Thank you ♥

With Love, Ella

Social Media

Instagram: @isabellag.poetry
Twitter: @IsabellaGPoetry
Tumbler: @isabellagpoetry

Made in United States
North Haven, CT
03 October 2022